Our Identity

A Book
by
Robert L. Harris

HATCHBACK Publishing
Genesee MI

Our Identity
©2018 Robert L. Harris

All Rights Reserved. No parts of this publication may be reproduced or transmitted in any form or by any means, electronic or mechanical, or any information storage or retrieval system, without prior permission of the publisher or author.

Published by
HATCHBACK Publishing
Genesee, Michigan 48437
Since 2005

The views, opinions and words expressed in this book are those of the author and do not necessarily reflect the position of HATCHBACK Publishing LLC or its owners

ISBN 978-1-948708-20-3

Printed in USA
10 9 8 7 6 5 4 3 2 1

For Worldwide Distribution

CONTENTS

1. Our Identity..............................5
2. Who Are You?...........................9
3. Important You..........................13
4. Character Assassination................17
5. A Part of the Past......................21
6. Heritage...............................25
7. Passing on Family Values..............31
8. Family Reunions......................37
9. Our Roots............................39

Closing..................................43

ONE

Our Identity

When we're born, we know nothing about our history, or the background of our descendants. At first, we could not care less, as we are spared the act of wondering who we are. When we were young, we have few curiosities regarding this. As children, we lived in a child's world, with a child's heart. All we knew then was to be a kid and go along with whatever was happening at the time. So, in our early lives, there isn't much need to understand our mother, father, or grandparents. We simply understand our parents as mom and dad. The questionings may come later. It is wonderful to be younger because there is no need to be concerned about our history, or the background of people we come from. We are born into a family. We are a product of our parents, our parents are a product of theirs, and so on.

The truth may be that your fate is already laid out according to your genetic makeup, whether good, bad, of whom we come from. There's little you can do about it, except try to understand, and work with that fact. Hopefully you come from a good source of people. You may learn some of the answers by observing present and past relatives and by looking at overall character traits. What you find may be indications of what you should realize. Take it from there, whether good or bad, then paint your own portrait. To understand is the first step and to cope with it is the second. Then to be honest with your findings is third. If you like what you have come up with, all you have to do is work within the framework of what you believe to be good. You should have a sense of pride you have that foundation laid out for yourself. Be appreciative of that fact and do your part to keep it going. Just as they did it for you, you owe it to your followers to do the same. We had nothing to do with whatever our ancestors did, or how they were. You need to understand whatever you can about them.

When you were born, you became another branch of the family tree. There's more to you than just you. Identity recognition is what we all want. It may take time to understand the person you are.

Some people don't know who they are. Reasons may be they never bothered to find out, or they don't care. I believe that it's important to know as much as possible about you family history. It may help you better understand yourself.

TWO

Who Are You?

Who you are is everything about you. You are the son or daughter of your parents. If you have brothers or sisters, you are either the oldest, youngest or middle child of your siblings. If you have kids, you are a parent. You may be a grandparent. You are the person of whatever accomplishment you have achieved. If you were in the service, then you are a veteran. If you have any special skills or talents, that's who you are. If you have any relative that may be famous or a high-profile person, they are also a part of you. You may be the parent of a gifted child. One of your ancestors may have been an important person. You are the person of what material things you have. Whatever education you have or award you have received, that's you. Whether you work at a job or you are an entrepreneur in business, that's you. If you belong to an organization, that's who you are. If you have ever done anything that was amazing, that's a part of who you are. How you are received by others is an indication of who you are.

I believe if you ask some people who they are, they can't tell you. Some don't give it much thought. They may feel it is unimportant or they may be young and not understand it is best to know as much about their background as they can. Some people may come up with many negative things about their origin. Some don't look for or realize there could be many good things in their family's background. Some drown in their own sorrow.

Believing the worst, many use this as an excuse when they should realize if you fall short of what is expected of you, you only have yourself to blame. They look for the nearest escape. For some reason they don't see themselves as man or woman enough to take on life. It's in their minds that they don't measure up, so they don't aspire to do much. Some may not realize they are most responsible for their own disappointments. They never really tried to put their best foot forward and their life is in real crisis. It's bad to live this way, especially if people before you were accomplished. You just are not doing your part.

Since the beginning, people have always used excuses for their failures. These are pitiful souls. Some may have the capability but lack the drive. A steam engine does not fuel itself. Someone has to do that. Once fueled, it runs great. Unlike a steam engine, you must fuel yourself. You may run great but if you wait for someone else to do this, you may never take off. In most of our lives, there is good as well as bad. If you have no desire to search for the good, you are stuck with the bad. Some may try to crack a walnut without a nut cracker and may give up, but if all else fails…use a hammer!

THREE

Important You

Some people may be more important than they realize. The fact that they may not know and understand they are, may be what's wrong. It's my belief most people have something special about them. They may not know how to tap into it. Like unexplored territory, you will never know what's there until you try and find out. You may make all sorts of discoveries. The capabilities some people have may go to waste if they do nothing to put it to work for them. It's like having something nice no one ever sees. What good does it do you? Some people may not have someone that believes in them to help develop some of their potential. A mother or dad may see something special about a child, yet they do nothing to encourage that child to pursue it.

It's fortunate to have someone that cares enough to see and help you achieve the good things about yourself. If you don't happen to have someone like this, it is up to you to know that you may be something special. You must place importance on yourself. Don't wait for someone else to do this. If you don't think highly of yourself, you can't expect others to.

I know someone who is a mechanic, electrician, carpenter, and plumber. He is good at all of these things, yet this person places little importance on himself. In all his years, he has done work for many. The work he does, he only gets paid a third of what he should. One reason being, he undermines himself. He's never even had business cards that advertised his skills. Business cards would give a description of what he does and speak volumes for the talents he has. If I were him, I would pay top dollar for the best advertising cards I could find. Another reason he is underpaid is because he feels he is not certified and has no license. True, it's best to be certified because that can work greatly on his behalf. Even that being the case, this person should have pursued getting a license at any cost. The good work he does and the years he has put in, could allow him to be a licensed independent contractor. Thus, he would be able to charge more for his work, which would help make him whole. I am sure he would feel better about himself. He is the benefactor of a relative who taught him what he knows. But much of what he knows goes to waste simply because of his excuse of being unlicensed. He doesn't feel as good about himself as he should. He has special talents some wish they had. This is typical of someone that may not know the gifts they've been given or how to use them to the fullest potential. Why be tied to petty limitations. The relative that helped him passed on a legacy that was passed on to him as well.

Some people do things such as this. There is nothing worse than wasted talent. The talents you possess, some wish they had. Be all you can be and maximize your capabilities.

Many good things may have been passed on to us. It's up to us to realize that our genetic makeup may contain talents and capabilities that should be put to good use. It's up to the individual to know and understand what they may have already been given.

Look for some of the capabilities your relatives may have. You may possess what they are also good at. Your mother and father pass on things to you that were passed on to them from generations of your people. I'm sure some of these things may be awesome. You may have come from a long line of proud, talented, and productive people. If this is true, you need to keep it going. Pass this on to your peers. You owe it to yourself and family to keep and pass on what was passed on to you. If possible, enhance it. Sort out the bad and use the best.

FOUR
Character Assassination

Character assassination is an attempt to tarnish the reputation of a person. It may involve manipulation or misleading half-truths of a fact to present an untrue picture of the targeted person. It's a form of defamation and can be a form of a hominem argument. It is a deliberate attempt to destroy someone's good name.

Any time someone says something bad and untrue about you, they think and say what they believe to be true. This may not be the truth. According to what is being said, this may undermine your character and totally misrepresent who you are. Someone who barely knows you, may do this. The saying, *you can't judge a book by its cover,* many have heard but few abide by this. I once misjudged someone, not believing they had a black belt in karate. Take it from me, if someone tells you this, believe it. It takes a wise person not to waste time summing someone up.

It may be unfair, even harmful to talk about someone in a bad way. Get a life! It is true, however, many may stand in judgment. They perceive mainly what they think they see in a person or what someone has to say. It could even be what someone has. If somehow you don't measure up to someone's expectations, then they are evaluated. Unless someone correctly sees it, they may think and say things that hold little to no truth. They have summed the person up in their own way according to what they believe to be true. Unless this person has a change of mind or the person who is judged does something that changes it, they may think this way for all eternity.

A generation of good things that have been passed on to you. Your family's principles and values can all be taken away by character assassination. Being misjudged may change the dynamics of all the good things about you. It's like being accused and sentenced for a crime that you didn't commit. You should not allow this to happen. You should try and set the record straight. Do what's needed not to be misunderstood. Many people have been brought down this way. It seems a shame you can't be yourself, the way that is totally you. If someone has a false conception of what they perceive to be you, they very well may write your epithet. Write your own, for no one knows you better than you.

Gossip is one of the greatest ways to say things about a person that may not be true. People spend hours on the phone doing this, some may not have anything else to talk about other than someone else. For some, gossip is a way of life. These are the ones that keep mess going. They are the real character assassinators. Take note of the first three letters, "a-s-s!" You hear it all the time.

"He thinks he's something because he has a new car." The person being talked about may simply be happy to have a new car. Or, "Girl, did you see that dress she had on? Trying to look like she's twenty-five. She thinks she's a glamour girl, and she probably ain't got a dime!" The person being talked about may simply be happy she found a dress of the right color and it fits her curves nicely.

The truth is, we treat each other unfairly when we do such things. Sometimes the person being talked about is a really a nice person just trying to get through life the same as you or I. When we do this, it also undermines your character because you should have better things to do! Put the focus on you. Don't waste time on others. Don't be a faultfinder. Try and concentrate on your own faults. If you are a dynamic, successful individual, a born leader, highly charismatic, popular or attractive, at some point you are guaranteed to be the target of character assassination.

FIVE

A Part of the Past

We may live in the present, but we are still a part of the past and our family's background. Although we had nothing to do with anything, nevertheless we're still a part of that history. It must have been an adventure for Alex Haley to trace his family roots. Many people would love to do this, I know I would. If we could, we may be surprised at our findings. Nowadays, many people are tracing their family's history. Why? They want to know. What if you could discover you are descended from royalty, or your great-great grandfather was an inventor who helped changed things. It's possible, and you would be a part of that. Some things you find may be good, some may be bad. There's nothing any of us can do to change the past. We can only live in the present. The fact is, you come from a good or bad source of people.

Whatever the case, much was passed down to you.

I've often wondered how a person that's no good, a rotten person, would have the audacity to have children. Someone may be a serial rapist or killer. They may be ruthless and care nothing about anyone. They are an all-around bad person that has kids who have to live out that legacy. That kid may be persecuted all of their life because of what a parent did. It seems unfair, then again life may not be fair.

Kids need someone to look up to and admire. Maybe someone they would like to imitate, instead of some damn pedophile or mass murderer. It's my belief these people are selfish. They have no consideration for a child they bring into the world who has to live a life surrounded by all the crazy things their parent did. This is unfortunate for anyone. Some people are ashamed, have had to run, try and hide, or maybe change their identity all together because of a parent. We can't choose our parents, we can only live in their shadow.

I had a friend who detested his father. It was past the point of dislike. I saw firsthand the disappointment he had in his dad. He was ashamed of him and everyone knew this. I saw what it did to my friend. He would change in the worst way when he was around his dad. Although his dad was no mass murder or rapist, he was a sloppy drunk who did crazy things. He didn't seem to care about the bad impression he made. This ate away at my friend like cancer. Although he was a good person, my friend would fall to pieces because of his dad. The dad, because of his ways, offset the way my friend wanted to feel about his dad. He changed from the person he was to the person he didn't want to be. The dad assassinated his son's true character.

Who doesn't want a dad they can be proud of? Once you bring a child into this world, you owe them. They didn't ask to come here. You as a parent are indebted to them. They do not owe you. So, it is up to you to do all you can to make that child proud of you. You are unworthy of your life, if you are not worthy of your kids. Consider them a project you are going to complete.

Be a mission man, do what a mission man does.

SIX

Heritage

We all have been given our heritage. Some have inherited poverty and suffering. Heritage is a cultural aspect of tradition that has been passed down through generations. What has been passed down to you could be good or bad, wealth, poverty, crazy behavior, or scholarly thinking. You have been given either a gift or a bill you may have to pay for. Sad to say, not all may be good. You are either fortunate or not in that respect.

We all come from a long line of our people before us. Some people live in the shadow of bad things and the history of ancestors. Just as one may come from people who were fine and upstanding, some come from a line of people who were of poor character that passed down things people in the present are paying for. A person may not understand why they do the things they do or they don't understand themselves. They may not understand their heritage is calling. If you come from a long line of wife beaters, it's likely you may be one yourself. If you were a kid and saw this, you may have been looking at yourself in the making. You now, "like father, like son." It's likely if you came from a long line of criminals, it's possible you may be one. If you conducted a study of people who are always in trouble, to be truthful, they may not be able to help themselves. Some have no resistance to fight off medieval spirits.

When I was growing up, I had a friend who basically was a nice guy. You could tell he wanted to be that way. I remember him trying to take pride in his schooling. He was concerned about his grades and homework. I remember him telling me he could not study at home because of all the chaos and madness that went on. My home was pretty much the same except for one fundamental difference. I had no criminal elements. I had no sisters or brothers always getting into trouble as he did. We argued over what to watch on TV. He argued about being left alone to do his homework. He fought hard to be different from his family. He wanted to make something of himself. I could clearly see this in him.

I felt a little sorry for my fried, although my young self knew what he was up against, I could almost see his outcome. It looked grim. Despite the efforts he put up, they were no match for the people he descended from. His dad was a career criminal who was in and out of jail. His mom, in her early days, transported money for the mob. He had two sisters who walked the streets. He had a brother serving time for armed robbery and his youngest brother did not want to go to school. He had uncles that always carried pistols and was a part of organized crime. How do you get away from all this? Eventually my friend started answering to his callings, and once he started, there was no stopping. He was within one semester from graduating, and dropped out of school, beginning criminal activities. Before long, he was in jail. Once he got out, he went for bigger crimes. He eventually killed someone and was sentenced to life. He served seven years only to be killed a year later.

It's a tragic story of how it may go if you happen to come from a source of bad people. However, it doesn't have to be all doom and gloom. You should know, like anything else, there is always an exception to the rule. If this is the case, you can change this if you want. You must realize unless you try and separate it, you are at the mercy of your bad heritage. It may lead you in directions you my not even want to go. Many have moved to other countries, changed their names, and did whatever they needed to do in attempt to hide. They may be ashamed of the family they come from. I give them credit for realizing they must do something. If they didn't, they may be a part of something that in the long run, destroys them.

We can't choose who we come from, we can only endure. If we could choose, I imagine we would be very selective, nothing but the best. Know and understand your heritage. Realizing it may help you do what you can to change some of it. Many people have been born into poverty, some except that and do little to change it. On the other hand, some refused to stay in it.

Just because my mom and dad were poor, they could not see themselves in the same way. The desire to not be poor drove them in directions that changed what might have been handed down to them... poverty. All of this could have been a reality for them. They refused to be broke, hungry and poor. It's the reason I say, it doesn't have to be all doom and gloom. Make that change, you have one of four seasons to do so, winter, spring, summer or fall, you choose which.

SEVEN

Passing on Family Values

I think it's important that we pass on family values. The world has changed so much, it may be hard to think much on this. To some, it may seem unimportant because we may be too busy just trying to keep pace with this hectic life. This is not to say we have completely forgotten.

I believe years ago people thought more about their family's history. Nowadays people are so preoccupied with what's going on in the present, little thought is given to the past. We should never forget. We should remain curious about our origin. We should continue to pass this on from generation to generation.

In my day, you knew your grandparents on both sides. When I was young, my grandmother would tell me stories about her past, the people she came from and how it was back in her day. I was a good listener and found what she said fascinating. Though her I learned some of the things about my family I may have never known. She told me all about my mom, and how she was when she was a young girl. That helped me understand more about her. Grandparents back in the day seemed to feel an obligation to teach and pass on things they felt you should know. We knew all uncles, aunties, cousins, and anyone that was a relative, whether they lived near or far. We knew because our parents often talked about them. They never let you forget that you had an aunt or cousins in Georgia. When relatives would visit, the red carpet was rolled out for them. We anxiously awaited their arrival, it was an exciting time for all of us. We loved and in our own way, wanted to protect them. They seemed precious. I had female cousins that I wanted to keep away from my hoodlum friends, referred to nowadays as "thugs." I knew how they were. I didn't want to see my cousins with them.

Family values seemed more important back then. There was family love. Anyone that was kin was automatically loved, we didn't seem to look for anything bad about them. We simply accepted them as family and treated them as such. People should never forget or know what to place value on. Don't let all the crazy things that go on today, take that away. I think the trial and tribulations we face today may help do just that. Some people today don't know or even care about relatives. They may have kin they don't know anything about because no on tells them. Sad to say, these days we have relative rivalry like never before, cousins that don't like cousins, even brothers that don't like brothers. We have women that care more about a boyfriend than their own child. We have men of today that have child after child and aren't in their lives.

I worked with a guy who had a beautiful set of twin daughters. I asked if he ever saw them. His answer was I only pay child support because the mom and I don't get along. A man should not use this excuse, for it's a poor one. No doubt it's a man's responsibility to pay support, it's just as important to be a part of a child's life. A child raised without a father is like rowing a boat with only one paddle. All you have to be is male to produce a child, you have to be a man to raise one. We fall right into traps that may have been set for us. We can't see this and certainly can't understand.

The world today does not promote love, only reasons to hate. That stage has been set, deterioration of family may be the plot, and annihilation may be the result. In the grand scheme of things, you need to understand what's really going on. Don't help aid things that in the long run may destroy you. Many generations of people were destroyed, maybe because they were not unified. One needs to understand this and anyone who doesn't, I pity the fool.

We may only have each other if we have nothing else. We should learn to combine strengths, support each other, and not destroy a confidence. Maybe we should exchange good information, inspire when we can, and combine resources. It may be as simple as if you have a niece that graduates from high school, everyone should come together and congratulating her. Tell her how proud you are, and give her something to help her to aspire to clever thinking. These are ways to keep families going. Do your part even if others don't, pass the torch. Someone has to do this if you don't want your family history forgotten or fading away.

We must live through our past to get to the future. Everyone has a story; our story is our past. With that understood, do your part for a brighter future.

EIGHT
Family Reunions

Family reunions are a good thing. They help families to come and gather together for a common goal, to meet and greet. When you attend, you may see relatives you never knew you had. It's amazing to discover a first or second cousin you didn't know about. This could be made better if you happen to bond. It's interesting to talk with kin just to hear what they have to say. I've gone to a few and have always liked being there with all of my relatives. To see young people that have become branches of the family tree realizing it is they who must carry on.

Although some elders have passed, what they have left behind are children that must carry on. When children attend these functions, it may give them a chance to see relatives maybe for the first time. It gives everyone an opportunity to see they are a part of this group. They are a part of something bigger than themselves. These reunions help to keep families together, they are a symbol of unity, strength, and pride. It gives you a chance to see firsthand who your people are.

NINE
Our Roots

We all have roots of people from which we descended. Some might give little thought to this fact, nevertheless, our ancestors long before us paved the way for us to be here today. Our history goes back hundreds, even thousands of years.

Roots, the Series, gave millions a chance to see and know we came from many people before us. It opened the eyes of everyone. Many came to want to know about the history of their family. When it was on, I could hardly wait for the next episode. It was so interesting for me to see where it all began, and things people had to endure. I was able to understand that generation of people were subjected to the time of which they lived. I saw firsthand the price they paid just for us to be here today. To know, whether we realize or not, we were a part of that and will forever live in the shadow of it all.

I learned it is important to be true to yourself, which helps to make you the person you really are. I also learned you don't have to accept whatever may be your fate so long as you stand by the person you are. I love how Kunta Kinte, (one of the main characters) although in bondage, never gave up on who he was. They may have taken everything else, but what they couldn't take was his proud heritage that helped reassure people after him would know to believe in themselves. What he believed was passed on to his daughter, and she passed on things that kept the family going for generations after her.

We need only understand that we have been given all we need to know about us through our forefathers. It's up to us to do all we can so what they did to not be in vain. Sacrifices they made and doors that were closed to them, today may be opened to us. It's up to each of us to know we should respect our elders. They may know more about the family. Talk with them, ask questions, have an interest in learning all you can. We are not just here to live entirely in the present and forget our past. This may be open to your own interpretation, the past may be the key to understanding who we are.

Once you understand how, you may come to know why. Once you know why, you may then want to know who. It's only to your benefit for you to learn and use what's been given to you. Be the benefactor of the good handed down to you.

Closing

It's been my privilege to write about all of our past, which each and every one of us has. Hopefully I made someone aware of the importance to know and understand where we come from and who our forefathers were.

History is no more than things that occurred in the past which proceeds the future, the future is now and beyond. It's a shame people do not give recognition to all the things that came before us, for it is those things that help make us who we are today. Understanding your past may only help you understand the present.

Today, we still use sayings that may have been used by our grandparents.

The grass is not greener on the other side.
Fools rush in where wise men dare not go.
A hard head makes a soft ass.

Your grandparents may have used the same sayings year ago and they were passed on. We were given certain strength and knowledge we may often use and not know where they came from. Chances are they may have come from your great great-grandmother you may not have even known.

Have you ever heard anyone say, "I don't know where he gets his stubbornness from?" That stubbornness in you may have come from relatives long before you.

I was in a store and heard a lady tell her son, "You are just like your granddaddy." What an interesting comment. She didn't say, "You are just like your dad," which would have been perfectly understandable. I thought about what she said. She went back a generation to see her father in her son. Something he did reminded her of her dad. It helped me to see how things are passed on to us from generation to generation whether we realize it or not. When a father looks at his son, he may see himself, a duplication. A mother may see their daughters in the light of themselves. Who we are, are those who produced us.

When I was a kid, I noticed my mom seemed to be a perfect replica of her mom.

They seemed to be one in the same. I find it all amazing as I'm sure some may feel the same. God only knows how far back we may go.

Although he did a great job, Alex Haley could only go back so far. All that we come from is a mystery that we may never know. We were created and molded in images of our people long before us. We are descended from each and every one of our relatives, alive or dead. Just realizing this should give meaning and purpose to our lives. We are indebted to all our family, they may have served us well.

In your mind and heart, you should build a monument for them, because if there was no them, there would be no us.

www.ingramcontent.com/pod-product-compliance
Lightning Source LLC
Chambersburg PA
CBHW070749050426
42449CB00010B/2395